# DINO TO DOT

Published in 2016 by: Spirit Marketing, LLC
700 Broadway Boulevard, Suite 101, Kansas City, MO 64105
www.HelloSpiritMarketing.com © 2016 Spirit Marketing

 ISBN: 978-0-9965998-9-4

Designed in Kansas City by Chris Evans, Patrick Sullivan, and Chris Simmons.

For information about custom editions, special sales, and premium and corporate purchases, please contact Spirit Marketing at info@hellospiritmail.com or 1.888.288.3972.

Printed 5/16 in China

# DRAW-A-DINO

**FOLLOW ALONG WITH THE STEPS TO DRAW YOUR DINOSAUR.**

## PACHYCEPHALOSAURUS

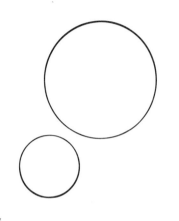

**STEP 1**

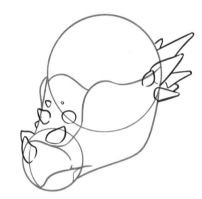

**STEP 4**

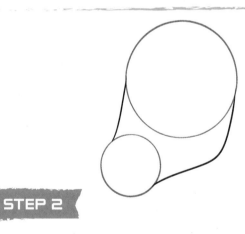

**STEP 2**

**STEP 5**

**STEP 3**

**STEP 6**

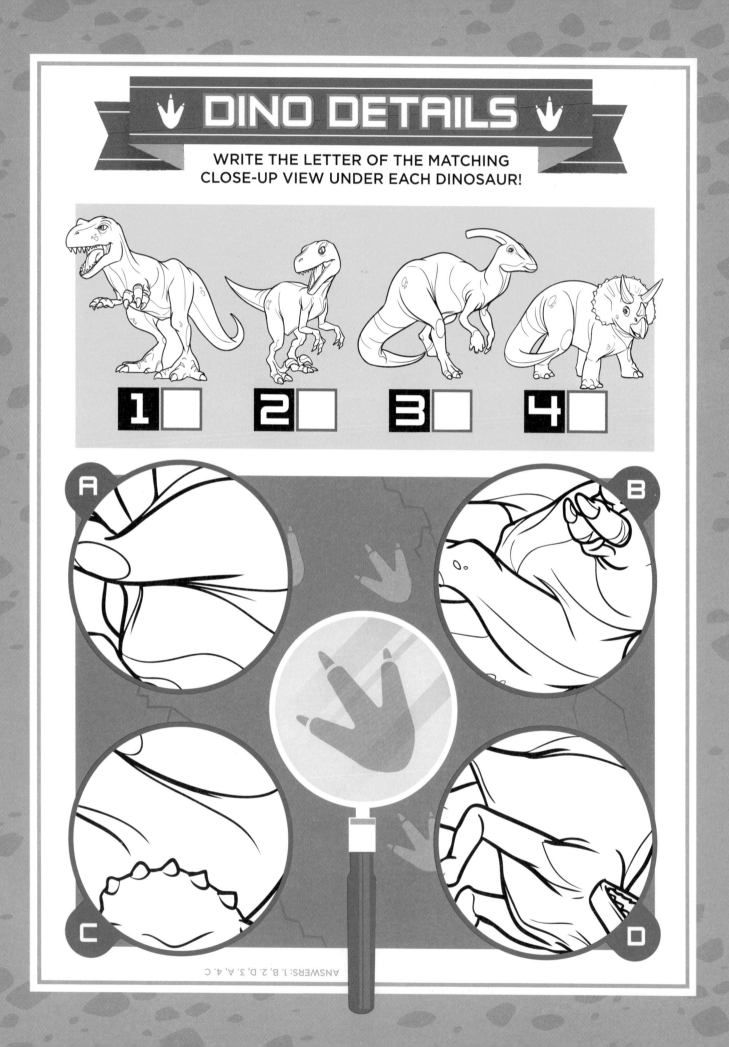

# DINO DETAILS

WRITE THE LETTER OF THE MATCHING
CLOSE-UP VIEW UNDER EACH DINOSAUR!

1 ☐  2 ☐  3 ☐  4 ☐

A

B

C

D

# PARASAUROLOPHUS

(PAH-RAH-SORE-O-LOE-FUS)

# DINOSCAPE

CREATE YOUR OWN CUSTOM DINOSAUR SCENE HERE.
(YOU CAN USE THE STICKERS FROM THE BACK OF THIS BOOK.)

# ANKYLOSAURUS

(AN-KIE-LO-SORE-US)

# VELOCIRAPTOR

(VELL-OSS-E-RAP-TOR)

# TIC-TAC-ASAURUS

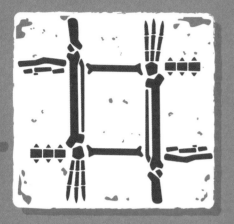
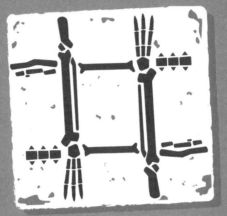
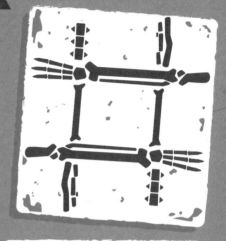
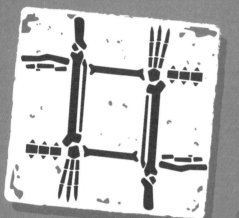
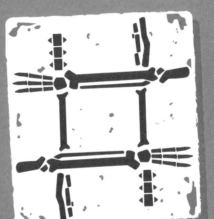
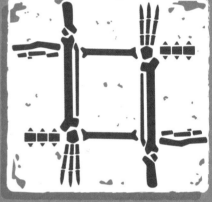

## JURASSIC JOKES

**Q** WHAT DID THE DINOSAUR SAY WHEN HE STUBBED HIS TOE?
**A** "IT'S DINO-SORE!"

**Q** WHAT DO DINOSAURS USE TO CUT DOWN TREES?
**A** DINOSAWS!

**Q** WHAT DO YOU CALL A FOSSIL THAT DOESN'T WANT TO WORK?
**A** LAZY BONES!

**Q** WHAT DO YOU GET IF YOU CROSS A DINOSAUR WITH A PIG?
**A** JURASSIC PORK!

**Q** WHAT DO DINOSAURS PUT ON THEIR PIZZA?
**A** TOMATO-SAURUS!

# DRAW-A-DINO

**FOLLOW ALONG WITH THE STEPS TO DRAW YOUR DINOSAUR.**

## TYRANNOSAURUS

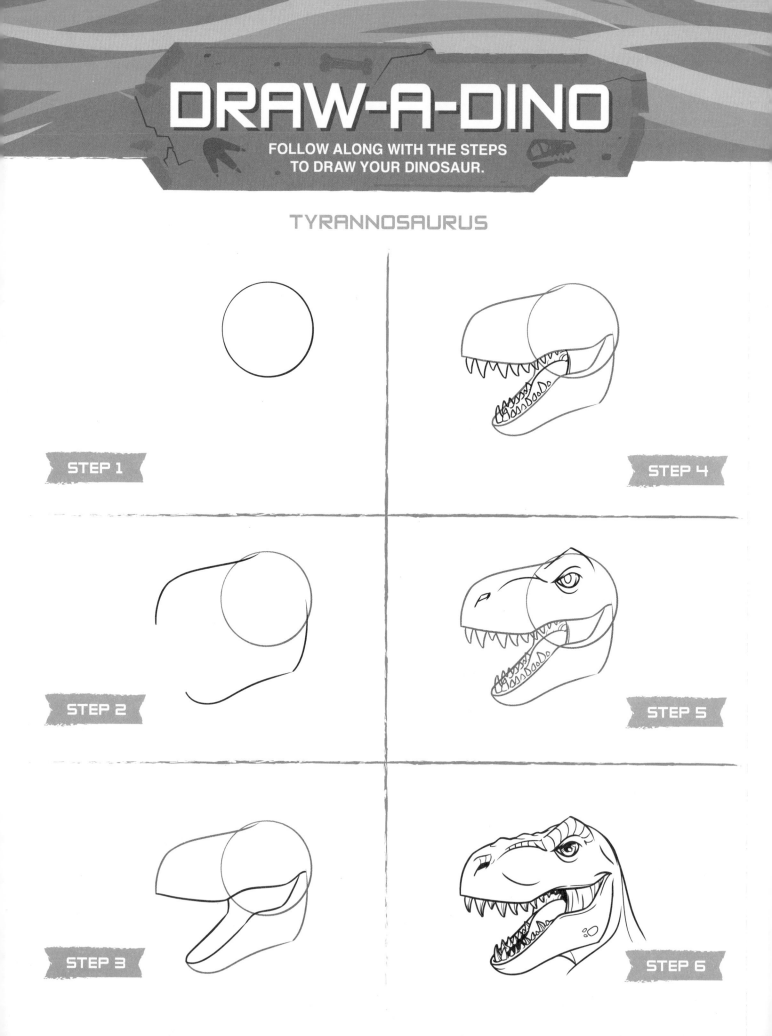

STEP 1

STEP 2

STEP 3

STEP 4

STEP 5

STEP 6

# DINO-SCRAMBLE

CAN YOU UNSCRAMBLE THE WORDS BELOW TO SPELL OUT WORDS RELATED TO DINOSAURS?

CJASURSI 1

APRORT 2

ECTXTIN 3

OSFSLI 4

WGINS 5

NODISURA 6

ATIL 7

LACWS 8

ABKE 9

USLKL 10

NHROS 11

ANSWERS: 1. JURASSIC, 2. RAPTOR, 3. EXTINCT, 4. FOSSIL, 5. WINGS, 6. DINOSAUR, 7. TAIL, 8. CLAWS, 9. BEAK, 10. SKULL, 11. HORNS

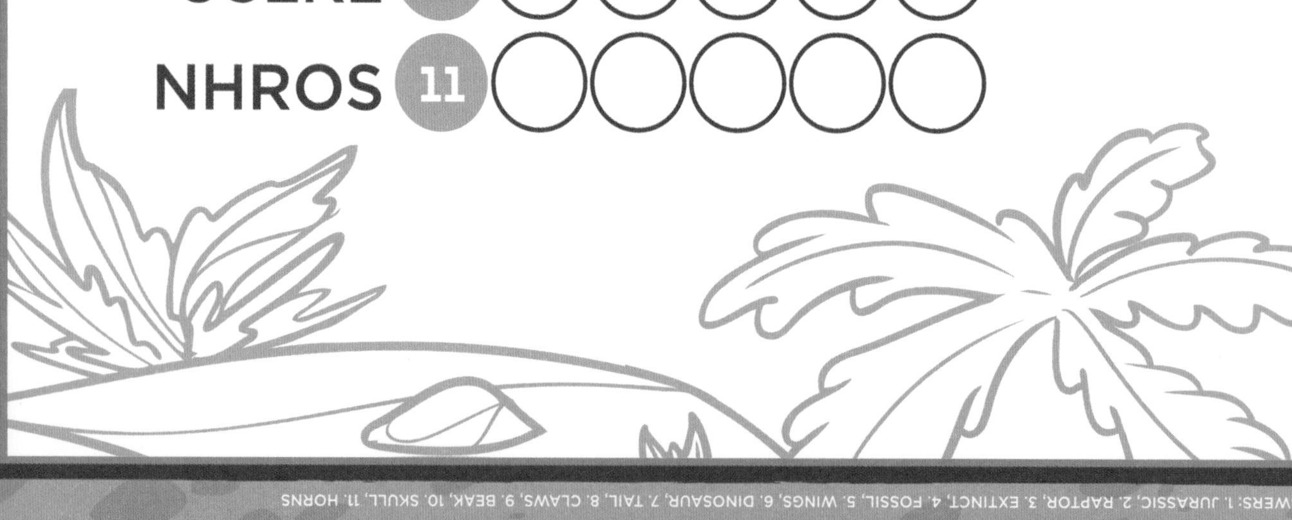

# TRICERATOPS

(TRI-SEH-RAH-TOPS)

# DINO-DISCOVER

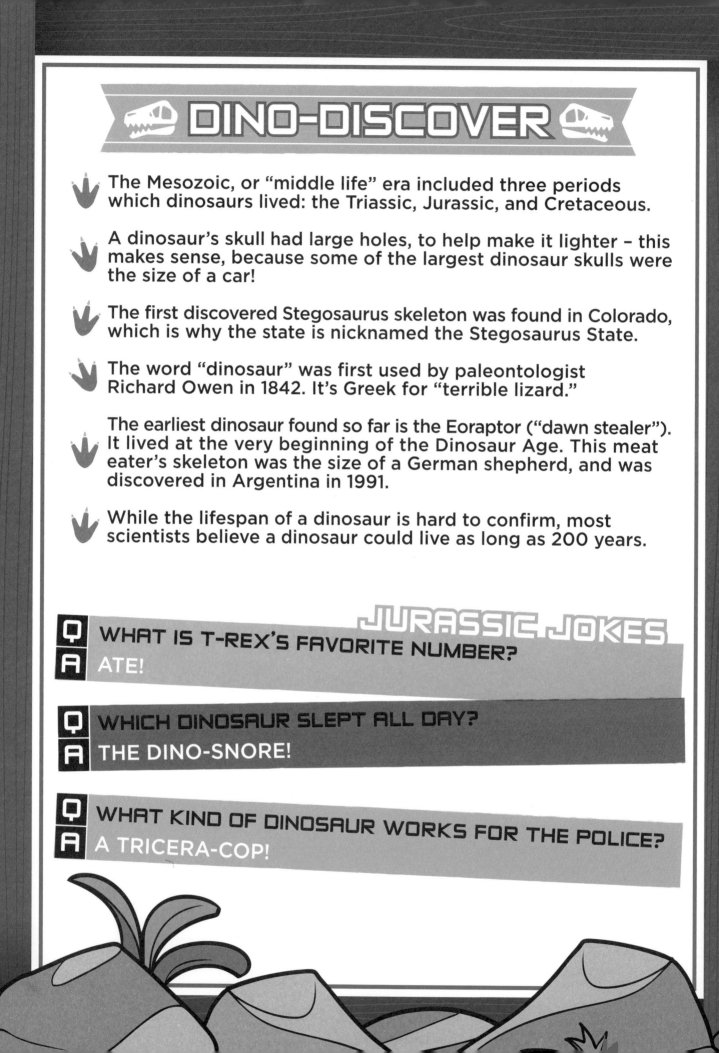

- The Mesozoic, or "middle life" era included three periods which dinosaurs lived: the Triassic, Jurassic, and Cretaceous.

- A dinosaur's skull had large holes, to help make it lighter – this makes sense, because some of the largest dinosaur skulls were the size of a car!

- The first discovered Stegosaurus skeleton was found in Colorado, which is why the state is nicknamed the Stegosaurus State.

- The word "dinosaur" was first used by paleontologist Richard Owen in 1842. It's Greek for "terrible lizard."

- The earliest dinosaur found so far is the Eoraptor ("dawn stealer"). It lived at the very beginning of the Dinosaur Age. This meat eater's skeleton was the size of a German shepherd, and was discovered in Argentina in 1991.

- While the lifespan of a dinosaur is hard to confirm, most scientists believe a dinosaur could live as long as 200 years.

## JURASSIC JOKES

**Q** WHAT IS T-REX'S FAVORITE NUMBER?
**A** ATE!

**Q** WHICH DINOSAUR SLEPT ALL DAY?
**A** THE DINO-SNORE!

**Q** WHAT KIND OF DINOSAUR WORKS FOR THE POLICE?
**A** A TRICERA-COP!

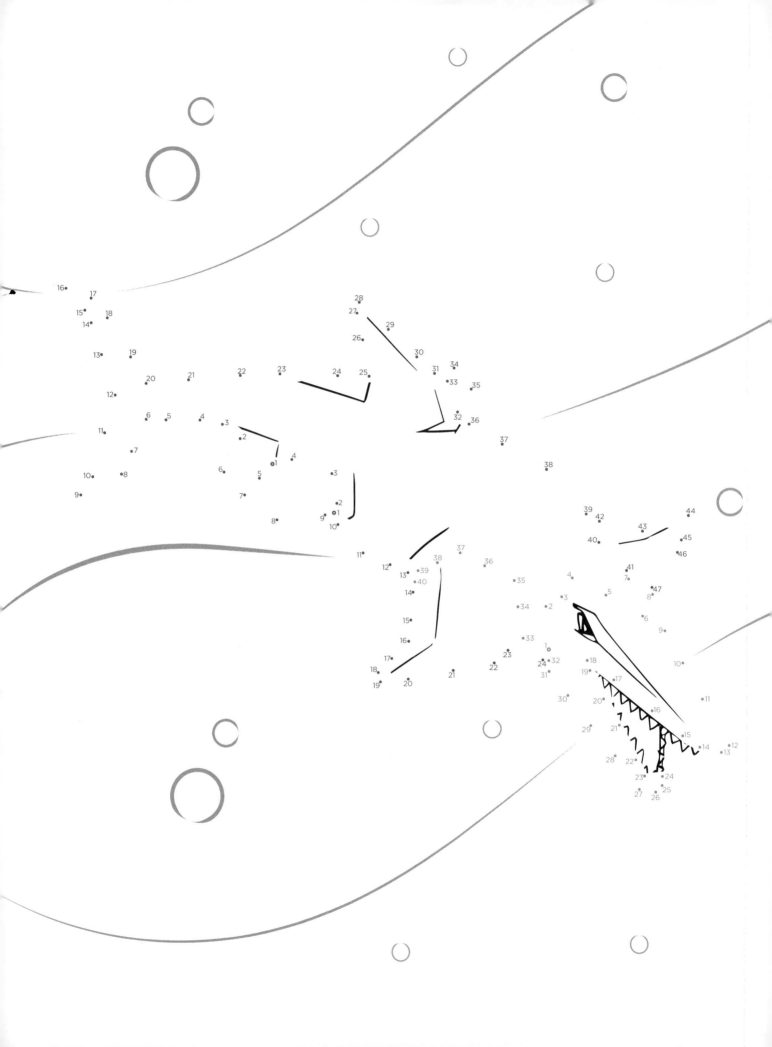

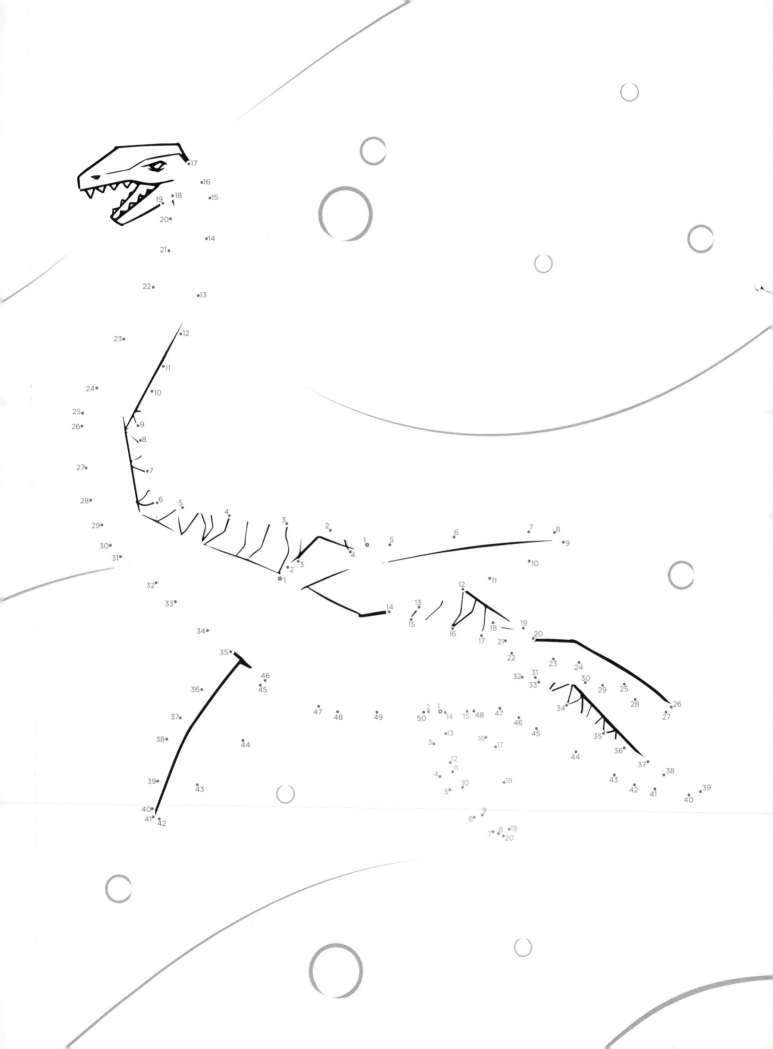

# BRONTOSAURUS

(BRON-TOE-SOR-US)

# STEGOSAURUS

(STEG-OH-SORE-US)

# MARSH MAZE

START

FINISH

# DRAW-A-DINO

**FOLLOW ALONG WITH THE STEPS TO DRAW YOUR DINOSAUR.**

## PARASAUROLOPHUS

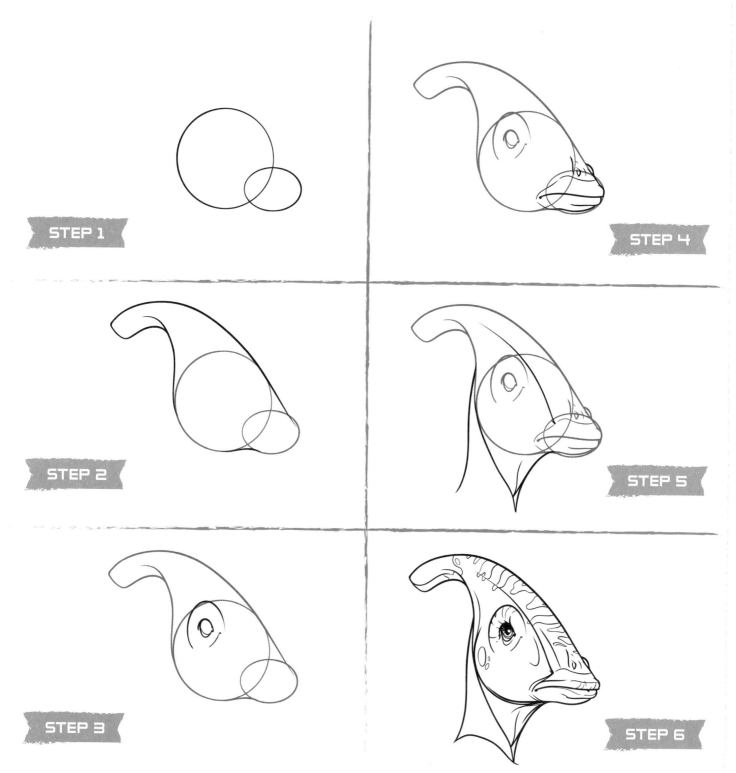

STEP 1

STEP 2

STEP 3

STEP 4

STEP 5

STEP 6

# WORD SEARCH-ASAURUS

```
A E C F Q G F E O M L K B Q
B M L K U A S C A L E S C E
D H O J P F G A Q C K E A M
C L A W S K G K U L J Q B H
C Q C E L J O A E C F Q D F
A U L M U S K U L L T N I O
F P O Y W O A E C A G S R O
E B M L K U C T E E T H Q T
A A B Z V X D H O J P O U P
T B O G C R E S T M A R P R
H D N A E C F Q E X B N F I
E E E C A G S R M A D S K N
R M S Y E G G S H Q C M J T
D H B M L K B E L B M L K U
H F O S S I L M J O A E A M
```

**FIND THE DINO WORDS HIDDEN TO THE LEFT**

- ○ CLAWS
- ○ TEETH
- ○ BONES
- ○ SCALES
- ○ HORNS
- ○ SKULL
- ○ EGGS
- ○ FOSSIL
- ○ FOOTPRINT
- ○ FEATHER
- ○ CREST

# DINO EGG DETAILS

**MATCH THE RIGHT PICTURES WITH THE ONES BELOW.**

A  B  C  D

1  2  3  4

# PTERODACTYLUS

(TEH-ROE-DACK-TILL-US)

# DINOSCAPE

CREATE YOUR OWN CUSTOM DINOSAUR SCENE HERE.
(YOU CAN USE THE STICKERS FROM THE BACK OF THIS BOOK.)

# SPINOSAURUS

(SPINE-OH-SORE-US)

# TYRANNOSAURUS

(TY-RAN-NO-SORE-US)

Archaeologists have to use particular tools to excavate their sites. Some of these tools are very expensive, and some are very common and inexpensive. Exactly what tools are used depends on the size, location and type of soil on each site, and what is being dug up.

# DRAW-A-DINO

FOLLOW ALONG WITH THE STEPS
TO DRAW YOUR DINOSAUR.

## TRICERATOPS

STEP 1

STEP 2

STEP 3

STEP 4

STEP 5

STEP 6

# DINO DOTS

You'll need two players. Take turns connecting the dots. When you complete a box, place your initials in it and take another turn. Keep taking turns until there are no moves left. The player with the most boxes wins the game.

# PLESIOSAURUS

(PLEH-SEE-OH-SORE-US)

# DINO-DISCOVER

- Dinosaurs were reptiles that roamed the Earth anywhere from 230 million years ago to 65 million years ago.

- Theropods, or meat-eating dinosaurs, meant "beast-footed" because of their sharp, hooked claws on their toes. Just the opposite, plant-eating dinosaurs had blunt hooves or toenails.

- It's estimated there were more than 1,000 different species of non-flying dinosaurs.

- Most people picture the dinosaurs as huge, but the majority of them were human-sized or smaller. More fossils of large dinosaurs are found probably because their bigger bones fossilized easier.

- Its fossils found in China, the dinosaur with one of the longest name is Micropachycephalosaurus ("small thick-headed lizard").

- Dinosaurs lived on all of the continents – even Antarctica.

- Some dinosaurs had long tails that helped keep their balance while running – some of the longest tails were 45 feet long!

## JURASSIC JOKES

**Q** WHAT DO YOU CALL A DINOSAUR THAT NEVER GIVES UP?
**A** TRY-TRY-TRY-CERATOPS!

**Q** WHAT DO DINOSAURS USE TO BUILD THEIR HOMES WITH?
**A** REP-TILES!

**Q** WHAT KIND OF DINOSAUR CAN YOU RIDE IN THE RODEO?
**A** A BRONCO-SAURUS!

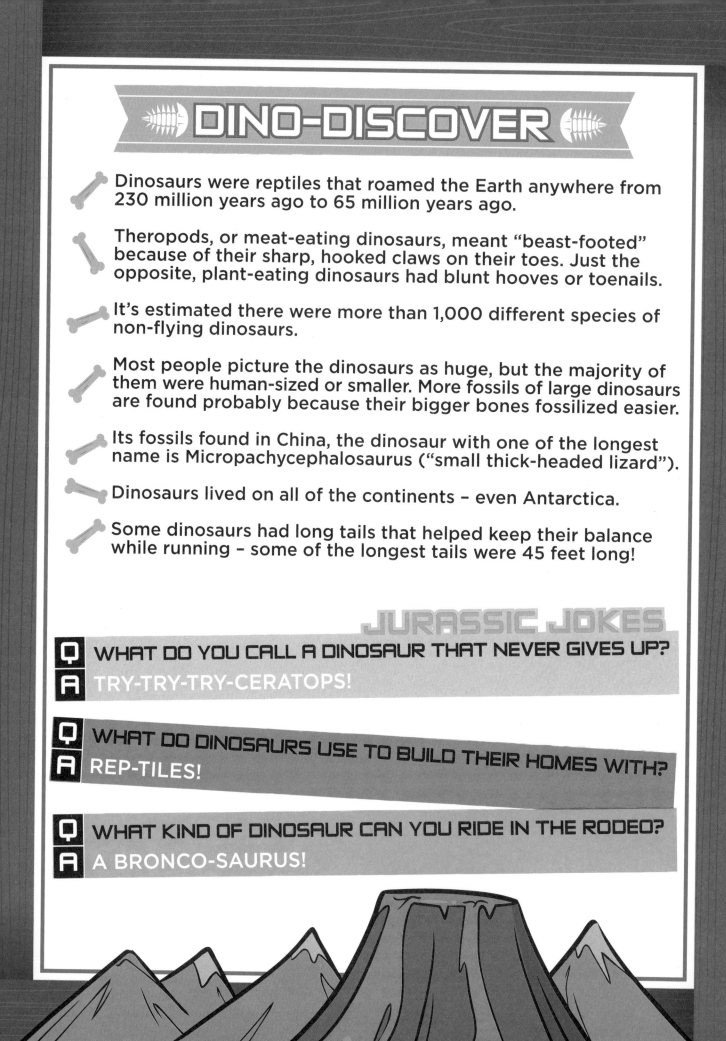

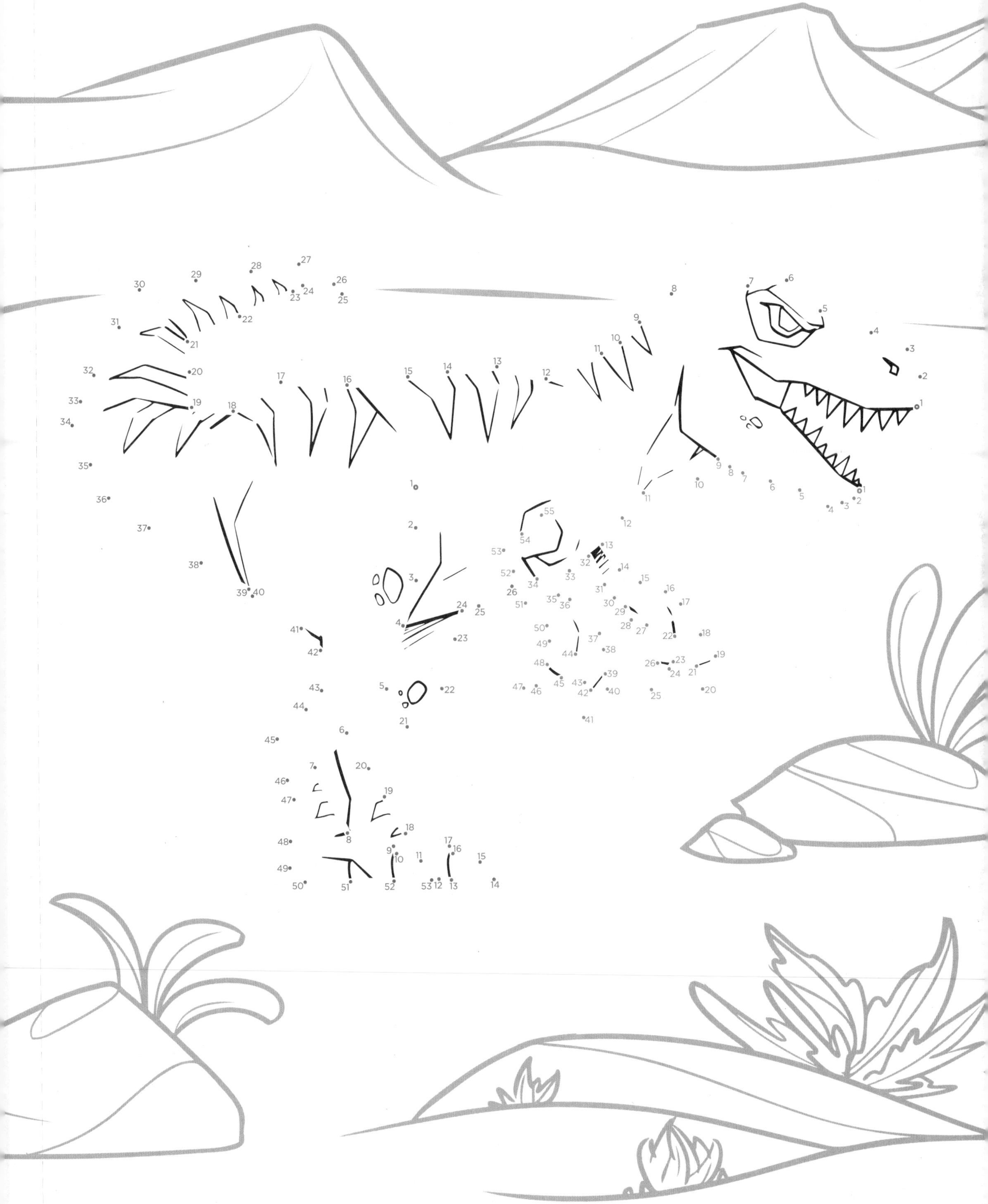

USE THESE STICKERS ON THE DINOSCAPE
PAGES OR ANYWHERE YOU LIKE.